"Fall Prevention: Planning Not To Fall is a fantastic resource for fall prevention. The stories are so relatable—I feel like I'm reading a script taken from the pages of the lives of many of my patients. I'll be recommending it to my patients, as they need this information before they fall or fall again. Consuela Marshall expertly explains the causes of falls and offers clear, practical steps to prevent them. An incredibly knowledgeable and easy-to-follow guide."

— Cassie J., MPT, Home Health Physical Therapist, Louisiana

I wish I'd had the WISE guidance Consuela Marshall delivers in *Fall Prevention: Planning Not To Fall* when I was a caregiver. As she breaks down in short, smart chapters, you can begin to find a foothold for yourself. I even changed a few of my own habits after reading this. Buy this book for yourself and share it with anyone you know facing caregiving challenges. It's powerful.

— Kitty Eisele, Emmy award-winning journalist and host of NPR's "24-7: A Podcast About Caregiving"

"I need this book. My parents are aging and doing well in their home. After reading *Fall Prevention: Planning Not To Fall,* I'm realizing I need to take action now to ensure they stay safe. I didn't know I should be making these changes before a fall happens."

— Joyce T., Caregiver

Kudos to Consuela Marshall for sharing her experience, knowledge and passion as an Occupational Therapist and long time caregiver in this important and easily understood safety handbook for patients, families and caregivers!! As an Occupational Therapist and caregiver myself, I found her safety tips to be very insightful and spot on. Consuela offers easy and simple, as well as cost effective solutions to the issues of safety and fall prevention. *Fall Prevention: Planning Not To Fall* is the perfect guidebook for and anyone in need of assistance in navigating the issues of safety in the home and community!

— Monique F., Occupational Therapist, Caregiver.

Marshall writes with the clarity of a healthcare professional but the warmth of a storyteller. The book never feels overly technical or bogged down with medical jargon. Instead, it reads like a conversation between friends, filled with humor, empathy, and deep wisdom. The stories are relatable and, at times, emotionally resonant, showing both the vulnerability and resilience of her clients. I highly recommend for any ambulatory adult.

— **Joy Petty, MSPT, CHC, Owner of Santa Rosa Beach Physical Therapy, LLC**

FALL PREVENTION: PLANNING NOT TO FALL

FALL PREVENTION: PLANNING NOT TO FALL

Daily Tips and Real-Life Stories To Decrease Fall Risks and Improve Aging In Place

Consuela Marshall, OT, CAPS

DISCLAIMER

The information provided in this book is intended for educational purposes only and is not a substitute for professional medical advice, diagnosis, or treatment. Always seek the advice of your physician, healthcare provider, or qualified occupational therapist with any questions you may have regarding a medical condition or safety concerns. The author and publisher assume no responsibility for errors, omissions, or any outcomes related to the use of the information contained in this book. Individual circumstances vary, and readers should use discretion in implementing recommendations.

To the many patients who have welcomed me into your homes, allowing me to share my knowledge while enriching my life through the friendships, lessons, and insights you've so generously shared. You've helped shape my professional journey and my understanding of autonomy, resilience, and the beauty of aging.

And to the family caregivers who tirelessly support their loved ones—you are seen, deeply appreciated, and worthy of the highest honor.

CONTENTS

PREFACE

Throughout my 25+ years as a home health occupational therapist, I've seen firsthand how a single fall can change a person's life forever –and the lives of their families, with many family members instantly becoming caregivers. Many of the falls often result in severe injuries, such as hip fractures, shoulder fractures, and head trauma, with the onset of extended periods of pain and weakness. What saddens me the most is knowing these falls were preventable. Throughout my career, I've often thought their stories might have differed if individuals and their families had the right tools and information to allow them to be proactive in preventing falls.

This book is my way of offering that tool—a resource to empower aging older adults to make meaningful changes to reduce the risk of falls. I hope you see yourself in some of the real-life stories shared within these pages, recognizing how quickly a fall can happen when you are just doing life. These stories are shared to inspire you to become proactive and make changes to help you avoid the life-altering consequences of a fall.

I hope this book is also a practical tool for the adult children of aging parents. Their lives often become chaotic as they scramble to figure out how best to care for their loved ones. Navigating the challenge of preventing future falls while respecting their parents' autonomy can be overwhelming. This book offers practical advice and actionable steps to help guide you through these difficult decisions.

INTRODUCTION

Staying in your home as you age—known as "aging in place"—is a goal many older adults share. Many older adults want to remain in their homes, but many wait too late to start thinking about what it takes to do so safely. Safely living in your home doesn't just happen by wanting or wishing for it – it takes planning. Fall Prevention: Planning Not To Fall will guide you through practical tips and real-life stories, empowering you to make the necessary changes to reduce fall risks and be as independent as possible.

Embracing Change

Change is not always easy; it can even feel threatening. I desire that you use this book to empower you to recognize circumstances that place you at risk for a life-altering fall. Please know that adapting your home and habits to accommodate your evolving needs as you age doesn't mean losing control; it means taking charge of your future.

Expertise and Experience

With 25+ years of experience as a home health occupational therapist and certified aging-in-place specialist, I've entered thousands of homes. I've seen the struggles of many who remain in homes that do not allow them to function safely and have the best quality of life. I've also seen the positive impact that simple changes in the home environment can make, allowing many to improve their level of independence and avoid falling.

How to Use This Book

I've kept the tips concise and manageable so you won't feel overwhelmed. Read 1-2 tips a day, reflect on how they apply to your situation, and take notes on the actions you plan to take. I've provided space at the end of the book for you to take notes. The goal is to give you the tools to stay safe and independent without feeling pressured or rushed.

For Family Members

This book is also for you if you're an adult son/daughter with concerns about an aging parent still living in their home. I appreciate that you are searching for answers to support them in remaining in their home. Your concern is understandable, especially if you see areas of concern and if your parent has already had a fall.

This book can be a valuable tool to help you work together with your parent to create a safer living environment. Please encourage them to read the tips and use the stories and advice to facilitate open discussions about making necessary changes. Remember, the goal is to empower your parent to stay safe and independent while providing you with peace of mind.

FACT

Falling is not a normal part of aging.

TIP 1: INSTALL GRAB BARS IN BATHROOMS.

Why This Is Important:

The bathroom is where most falls occur in the home. Adding a grab bar is equivalent to having the outstretched hand of a strong, muscular person always present to hold onto, providing stability as you stand or step into the tub/shower, thus reducing the risk of falling. It is essential to install grab bars that screw into studs in the wall and refrain from purchasing suction grab bars. Suction grab bars can suddenly pop off the wall when needed most. Please note that towel bars, shower curtain rods, and toilet paper holders are not grab bars; they are not designed or installed to support your weight. When installed in the proper location, grab bars can prevent falls. The bars can be installed in various positions -- vertically, horizontally, and diagonally, and in many areas of the bathroom.

Real Life Story:

Mr. Joe, 83, is a widower who lived through The Depression. He is very strong-willed, knows what he wants, and doesn't mind sharing what's on his mind. Mr. Joe's health has declined significantly since his wife passed away three years ago. His daughter MaryBeth now assists him every evening after work, doing a lot to help prepare meals, do housework, and pay his bills. MaryBeth was tired and even beginning to have neck and back pain. Her doctor recommended she have surgery, but she continued to postpone it because no one else was available to help her care for her dad.

MaryBeth knew Mr. Joe was beginning to struggle in the shower. Fearing he would fall, she would sit outside his bathroom door; he would not allow her to enter to help. MaryBeth recommended that he install grab bars because she recently had them installed in her shower, as recommended by her occupational therapist. To avoid the cost of having them installed, Mr. Joe purchased suction-install grab bars instead.

One evening, Mr. Joe lost his balance while washing his legs. He put too much weight on the suction grab bar, and it popped off the wall. Down to the floor Mr. Joe went, sustaining a fractured rib. After a six-hour ER stay, Mr. Joe returned home with intense rib pain and bruises. He now agreed to have grab bars properly installed. And against his liking, caregivers were now required to assist with all personal care and household chores. Mr. Joe couldn't believe caregivers cost so much; he hoped he could get someone to be with him all day — for $25 a day. Marybeth was not surprise. She was relieved to find a male caregiver to help with his care. She scheduled her surgery.

Do you need to plan to install a grab bar?

Can you see the benefits of having a grab bar? Most small grab bars are less than $20. Who can help you buy and properly install the grab bar(s)? Write it down so you don't forget.

TIP 2: USE NON-SLIP MATS IN THE BATHTUB OR SHOWER STALL.

Why This Is Important:

Mixing soap and water with a tile or tub surface is a perfect recipe for a fall. Using a non-slip mat in the bathtub or shower provides traction and reduces the risk of slipping. If you are saying that your tub already has a non-skid surface, you may have a false sense of security, especially if you have an old tub and the non-skid surface has worn down. Placing a non-slip mat in the tub/shower and a second mat temporarily on the floor directly outside the tub/shower are quick fixes. If you say you don't like those mats because they get moldy, I've got a remedy for that —take them up, turn them over, and hang them to dry after each use. An alternate suggestion is to place wide adhesive non-skid strips in the bottom of the tub/shower. Slipping in the shower is no laughing matter, even if you are lucky enough to have a handsome young fireman come pick your naked body up off the floor. Falls in the tub/shower can result in serious injuries.

Real Life Story:

Sally, 80, still driving short distances, loved to get her hair done every Friday. She had great pride in her looks and often bragged that she got her hair dyed "Lucille Ball Red" every six weeks. Sally cherished the weekly talks with her hairdresser and "the ladies" who exaggerated their adventures. She loved her weekly routine and made sure nothing interrupted her plans.

Sally was divorced and lived alone. She insisted on doing all her housework and refused to hire a caregiver or housekeeper because, after all, she didn't need help. Her son was very concerned about her and repeatedly tried to convince her to hire her unemployed neighbor to help. She always refused and often joked that she needed a handsome, strong man to move in.

While showering early one Friday morning, preparing to leave for her hair appointment, Sally slipped in the shower. (There was no non-skid surface.) "My feet just got from under me," she said. She sustained an arm fracture. She underwent a long recovery, with an extended hospital and rehab stay, causing her to miss several of her hair appointments.

Her son had a walk-in shower, with non-skid flooring, installed while Ms. Sally was in the hospital. He also hired the neighbor, a single mom, who helped around the house and now drove Ms. Sally to her hair appointments. Ms. Sally admitted she enjoyed the help. She was so glad to be back at the hairdresser, have her white roots colored again, and tell everyone the tall tale about her shenanigans in the hospital with one of her new "beaus".

Do you need to plan to purchase a non-skid mat?

Can you see the benefits of having a non-skid surface in your tub or shower stall? Decreasing your fall risk can be achieved for less than $20. Who can order or pick this up for you? Are you going to the store soon? Write it down so you don't forget.

TIP 3: RAISE THE HEIGHT OF LOW TOILETS.

Why This Is Important:

I know we've already had a couple of tips about the fall risks in the bathroom because most falls that happen in the home occur in the bathroom. In addition to falls occurring during bathing, a high percentage of them occur related to toileting. Some homes have low toilets, which can make it challenging to get on and off. Are you clawing and pulling to get off the toilet or going down so far to sit that it feels like you are sinking through the floor? Do you rock and count to get up? Struggles to get off the toilet can happen if you are tall, have weakness, or suffer from pain/stiffness in your hips, knees, or ankles. There are various options to remedy this problem.

Real-Life Story:

Ms. Mary has struggled lately with getting off the toilet due to arthritis in both knees. She used to get shots in her knees, but they no longer work to decrease the pain, and she refuses knee replacement surgeries after seeing her brother's complications with his knee surgery.

Ms. Mary's toilet has started to rock back and forth because she plops down hard on the low toilet, loosening the bolts that hold it in place. She often sits for extended time on the toilet after "finishing her business", applying green rubbing alcohol on her knees, swearing that it helps to numb the knee pain.

Ms. Mary's daughter is concerned; she noticed the toilet paper holder was broken. The daughter also saw the holes in the wall where a towel rack used to be. She knows that her mom has broken these things by pulling on them to help her get off the toilet. Her daughter becomes anxiouswhenever her mom calls her phone or if her mom doesn't answer the phone, continually fearing that her mom is on the floor in the bathroom.

Erroneously, the daughter believes that a complete bathroom remodel is the only solution, which is impossible with Ms. Mary's small Social Security check. Both mom and daughter hope a fall does not occur, though neither has done anything to make toileting more accessible and safer.

Do you need a plan to ensure that you can safely get on and off the toilet?

Can you see the benefits of raising the height of a low toilet? Can you see that the low height can cause you to struggle to get on and off it? Be aware that if the toilet is rocking and separating from the floor, the entire toilet can fall over, causing a huge problem.

If the toilet is stable, you can add height to it by adding a lock-in-place toilet riser with armrests or placing a bedside commode frame over the toilet. And if you add a grab bar to the wall, it can provide another level of safety.

Not all bathroom modifications are costly. The options mentioned above can cost less than $200. Of course, you can also buy a taller toilet and have someone install it, along with the grab bar. An occupational therapist can help provide the best option for your budget. What are your thoughts? Who can help you? Write it down so you don't forget.

TIP 4: ENSURE GOOD LIGHTING THROUGHOUT THE HOUSE.

Why This Is Important:

Dim lighting is one of the number one causes of falls in the home. Even if you think your vision is good enough and have a pretty good idea of where everything is located in your home, please don't skip this tip. Do you realize you can get used to "dim" and not even realize how dark your world has become? Yes, you may be seeing just enough to "get by" but not seeing what you don't see, and this is when a fall can happen. Falls can occur when you can't see where you are going or when something is out of place, and you just don't realize it. Living in a dark home can also dim your mood, causing you to move less and weaken.

Simply replacing old incandescent or CFL bulbs with LED bulbs can significantly improve the lighting in your home without breaking the bank—Brighten up your home and your mood with good lighting. Well-lit spaces help you see potential hazards and navigate your surroundings safely, reducing the risk of falls.

Real Life Story:

Mr. Johnson, a retired engineer, was a very organized person. He had a place in his home for everything. His workshop was also spotless; Mr. Johnson could instantly locate every tool, nut, and bolt he owned. He prided himself on knowing every corner of the home he built in the 60s. When given an opportunity, Mr. Johnson told anyone who would listen about how he did all the carpentry work, all the brickwork, and all the electrical wiring in his home.

One evening, while walking down his dimly lit hallway, Mr. Johnson tripped on something he had unknowingly dropped earlier that day and had a fall. He was so upset with himself because he had never fallen in his home before. He said, "I used to think that only careless people fall and that I knew better." Fortunately, he only suffered minor bruises, but it was a wake-up call for him to improve the lighting in his home.

Mr. Johnson now had a new project. He created a flowchart on how he would upgrade all the light bulbs in his house to LED and replace the old fluorescent lights in his workshop. "There is no point in half-doing things; I may as well get it all taken care of at once. I didn't realize how dark it was around here."

Do you need to plan to upgrade the lighting in your home?

Can you see the benefits of improving the lighting in your home? Improving the lighting in your home can be achieved gradually, starting in rooms you use often first. Decreasing this fall risk is a low-budget fix. Who can order or pick new lighting up for you? Who can help you change out the bulbs? Are you going to the store soon? Write it down so you don't forget.

TIP 5: KEEP PATHWAYS CLEAR OF CLUTTER AND OBSTACLES.

Why This Is Important:

Clutter can happen slowly; you don't plan for it to happen, and often, you can become blind to clutter all around. You can see the clutter and keep thinking, "I'll move all that stuff tomorrow," but never seem to stop to do it. Don't be that way. Clear pathways are like open roads to safety. When navigating through a room cluttered with obstacles, you're inviting trips and falls to occur.

Are those old newspapers on the floor next to where you sit for your morning coffee and cereal? Is that a pile of junk mail on the floor next to the toilet? Next to your bed? By the recliner? Are you truthfully planning to read all of that? These are hazards that put you at risk for falls. By removing clutter and maintaining clear paths, you minimize the risk of tripping, ensuring a safer, more navigable home environment.

Real Life Story:

Ms. Claire, 70, is a part-time librarian. She loves to read and quickly reads a murder mystery book in three days. Ms. Claire is always cold, which she says is due to the blood-thinner medication she takes. She sits and reads while wrapped up in her favorite soft blanket, a gift for Christmas from her very first grandchild. The blanket is a collage of many photos of her and the grandchildren. She often stares at the pictures, wondering where the time has gone, longing for opportunities to spend more time with them. The blanket is extra long and touches the floor when she snuggles under it.

One day, she stood from the recliner to get something to drink. She didn't realize her foot was caught in the blanket and resting on a magazine. (The magazine had fallen from the crocheting magazines piled next to the recliner.) She took two steps, carrying a cup in one hand and a book in the other. Down to the floor Ms. Claire went, suffering a black eye and considerable bruising that covered the entire left side of her face. She looked like she had been in a fight with Tyson. Luckily, she can joke about it, telling everyone that her husband finally found a way to shut her up when she repeatedly tells him it is too cold in the house.

Do you need to plan a little time each day to declutter a pathway?

Can you see the benefits of keeping pathways clear of clutter and obstacles? Decluttering can be achieved gradually, starting in the areas in your immediate pathways. It costs nothing other than your pride, time, and several trips to the recycling bin. Who can help you? Is there someone, maybe a grandchild, who can come help make things safer for you? Remember, Rome wasn't built in a day. Start slowly, but start. Write down a few things that you can do right now.

FACT

Aging In Place:

Staying in your home as you get older is called aging in place. But many older adults and their families have concerns about safety, getting around, or other daily activities. Living at home as you age requires careful consideration and planning.

(National Institute on Aging, 2024)

TIP 6: REMOVE THROW RUGS.

Why This Is Important:

All throw rugs, especially those without rubber backing, are hazardous. When you are using a walker, the fall risks increase exponentially. Throw rugs without rubber backing can move when you step on them. Throw rugs with rubber backing can also be hazardous as they can tend to roll up when the tip of your shoe hits it around the edge just right or when the wheels of a walker come in contact with it. Remove all area rugs and throw rugs located in your traffic areas, or secure them in place, taping down all four sides. These falls happen quickly – your foot gets caught, and you go down. And in case you are thinking, "I know I won't fall; I've had that rug forever," just know —those are famous last words.

Real Life Story:

Did you know that throw rugs are like The Genie's Magic Carpet and can have you airborne? My mother fell victim to The Genie Magic Carpet a couple of times. She kept a rug on the floor in front of her stove because the tile floor was cold to her bare feet. The rug was multicolored and appeared to be something you would make using one of those toy potholder-maker machines. There was no rubber backing, and the rug always moved, so she constantly straightened it out with her feet. I warned her that she needed to get rid of the rug. Well, what do I know? I'm only a daughter.

One day, she was rushing to the sink to turn off the water, and when her foot touched the rug, she went down the floor, injuring her knee. Fortunately, it wasn't too bad of an injury, plus she would not go to the hospital for x-rays. She never told me about this fall—I heard about it through the grapevine.

She made excuses for the fall, saying that she forgot to go around the rug "that time" and that she knows how to avoid the rug from now on. She kept the rug on the floor, and I could do nothing about it. Guess What? She fell again; I was not surprised.

Do you need to plan to remove throw rugs from your home?

Can you see the benefits of removing throw rugs or securing area rugs to the floor? This tip only costs your time and some duct tape or two-sided tape.

Think about it. Sometimes, changing a mindset about how we feel about things is all that is needed to improve safety. Changing your mind and deciding to make a change is not an admission that you are wrong about anything; it shows that you are open to doing what it takes to make things safer. Take a look around. Do you have throw rugs in your home? What are your plans now? Write it down.

TIP 7: AVOID STAIRS IF POSSIBLE.

Why This Is Important:

Do you have stairs inside or outside your home? As a young family, having a home with stairs can pose hazards to small children, but often are no challenge for the parents. However, the once-easy stairs can become significant challenges with aging. Add handrails as your trusty sidekicks on stairways, giving you something to hold onto. Having the handrails on both sides of the stairs provides the maximum protection. If you have balance problems and are not safe going up and down stairs, even with handrails, you could have a big problem. Converting a room downstairs into a bedroom and adding a bathroom is one option to explore.

Real Life Story:

Ms. Doris lived alone in a small split-level house. Her husband died five years ago, and she wanted to remain in the home that he built for them, where they raised their children. Ms. Doris was a long-time viewer of HGTV, back when the shows were good, showing people with average real-world budgets for remodeling a house.

Her children wanted her to move in with one of them, noticing that it was getting difficult for her to go up and down the five steps leading to the level of the bedrooms. Ms. Doris refused; she liked her neighborhood, enjoyed the nearby stores, and her church was only two miles away. Ms. Doris also knew her children were right. She knew in her heart that going up and down the stairs was getting risky for her. Ms. Doris did the math; she counted the cost of her freedom and safety in her home. She decided instead to convert the unused formal dining room into her bedroom and enlarge the lower-level bathroom.

"It just made sense. We never used that dining room anymore; we are a 'paper plates' family that eat at the kitchen counter. I admit it was hard not to walk into my old bedroom anymore; it was a big adjustment, but it was the best decision I could have made. I knew I had to do this before I had a fall," she proudly said. *"My old bedroom is now a hangout place for all the grandchildren and all those great-grandkids. They go up there and play those video games and take pictures and videos of themselves. If the kids leave a mess up there, so be it. I won't deal with it; that's up to their mommas. Everything I need is right down here with me."* Smart lady!

Do you need a plan that helps you address the stairs into or inside your home?

Can you see the benefits of avoiding stairs when you have impaired balance? Can you see the benefits of having two handrails near steps to enter your home and stairs onto another level? Handrails can be easily installed by a professional and are generally a low-budget fix. If your home only has bedrooms on an upper level, consider converting a downstairs area or moving. What are your thoughts? Write them down so you don't forget.

TIP 8: USE A NIGHT LIGHT.

Why This Is Important:

Many falls occur during the night due to the lack of adequate lighting. If your mom was like mine, she always left the light on over the stove, the light under the vent hood. It does the job when you walk into the kitchen, getting a snack in the middle of the night. But what about other areas of the home? It is best to use a night light or other types of low lighting in the bedroom, bathroom, and hallways at night. If you say, "I only sleep in total darkness," I have a solution. The motion-sensor night light, which turns on and off automatically when you enter an area, is the best option for you. No more groping around in the dark or hitting your toe on things at night; it is not fun. And let's not talk about going to the bathroom in the middle of the night. Having to stop to turn on a lamp can mean the difference in whether or not you make it to the toilet in time.

Real Life Story:

> *Ms. Pauline, 64, takes fluid pills. Like clockwork, she finds herself going to the bathroom every night. Ms. Pauline does not like to turn on her bedside lamp on weekends; she does not want to awaken her two-year-old grandson, who sleeps between her and her husband every Friday and Saturday night. Her grandson sleeps like an octopus and has difficulty resting, but she loves it.*
>
> *Ms. Pauline has a night light she can use on the weekends but does not always remember to turn it on before bed. Once he is asleep, she has learned to slide out of the bed slowly to go to the bathroom, stopping and holding her*

breath if it looks like he will wake up.

One night, she lay still as long as she could and "had to go" really bad. Rushing in the dark to the bathroom as quickly as possible, Ms. Pauline tripped on a toy and hit the floor. Let's just say she had two "accidents" — a fall and a spill. Ms. Pauline spent the rest of the weekend in the recliner with ice on her swollen knee. In learning of the fall, her daughter came up with a quick remedy –she brought over a motion-sensor night light to keep plugged into the wall at all times, which turns on and off automatically. Quick thinking daughter, protect your weekend babysitter.

Do you need a plan that helps you address inadequate night lighting in your home?

Can you see the benefits of having a night light in your home? A night light adds an element of safety that can prevent you from having a fall or "accident" at night. Night lights are available at most stores for less than $10. They no longer look like a Christmas light plugged into the wall. They come in various styles that can complement your home decor. What are your thoughts? Will you consider adding them to your shopping list? How many do you need? Write it down so you don't forget.

TIP 9: WEAR NON-SKID SOCKS PROPERLY.

Why This Is Important:

Walking around your home with regular socks on, those that do not have a non-skid surface, may feel comfortable, but it places you at high risk for falls. Wearing rubber sole shoes is a great option, but if you prefer not to wear shoes in the house, you can wear socks with non-skid bottoms.

Beware that wearing non-skid socks does not automatically reduce fall risk; the socks must fit correctly. If the socks are too big, the non-skid part can migrate to the top of the foot when you walk, rotating the slippery portion under the bottom and placing you at risk for falls. Also, just so you'll know, the non-skid texture can wear off over time. If you have had the socks for years —wearing, washing, and drying them often, the non-skid texture wears down. Also, if you wear the socks multiple days in a row (yes, so many people do), the sock can initially fit properly but become loose, and your foot can start sliding inside the sock, leading to a fall.

Real Life Story:

Ms. Kitty, 63, was a small business owner. She and her daughter owned a pet grooming salon. Ms. Kitty loved her job and her loyal customers. She planned to work three more years and then retire in the home she worked hard to pay for. When at home, Ms. Kitty did not wear shoes inside. She learned from her daughter that wearing shoes inside brought toxins into her house.

Ms. Kitty was careful to always wear her non-skid socks and made sure she had a clean pair handy. She had two pairs, issued four years ago when hospitalized for back surgery. The socks had been worn, washed, and dried many times, causing the non-skid texture to wear off, and they now fit loosely.

One day, Ms. Kitty was rushing to reach her phone. In a split second, she slid on her hardwood floors and had a nasty fall, landing on her back. Ms. Kitty now had new back pain but, thankfully, did not need surgery. She, however, required physical therapy and could not return to work for three months.

Ms. Bonnie was grateful that her insurance paid for therapy and that she had purchased the supplemental policy her daughter had recommended. The physical therapist saw her worn-out non-skid socks and how they fit, and educated Ms. Kitty on the dangers posed by her socks. Ms. Kitty purchased new non-skid socks and shared this new information with her business partner. She and her daughter were a great team and always looked out for one another.

Do you need to plan to avoid slipping and falling by wearing non-skid socks properly?

Can you see the benefits of wearing non-skid socks? Can you see the importance of them fitting correctly and being in good condition? Check to see if you have a pair and if they are in good shape. Do you need to buy a couple of pairs? Write it down so you don't forget.

TIP 10: AVOID OVERREACHING.

Why This Is Important:

You have something called your center of gravity, which we all do —the point in our body where our weight is evenly distributed. You maintain your center of gravity when standing, walking, and doing tasks; your body automatically adjusts so you don't land on the floor. You can remain over your center when you reach forward to pick up something within arm's reach. But when you get too far away from your center of gravity, thinking you have a "Go-Go-Gadget" arm, you shift your center of gravity, increasing the risk of losing your balance and tipping over. Your ability to recover from these shifts diminishes as you age, especially if you already have balance issues. Moving closer to the object you need is always better, reducing the risk of unnecessary falls and injuries.

Real Life Story:

Mr. Edwards has diabetes and has neuropathy in his feet. It is hard for him to always know where his feet are. He uses a cane to help with his balance. Mr. Edwards manages to live alone and prides himself on still being able to work on his truck and use the riding lawn mower to cut his yard.

Mr. Edwards has a favorite flashlight; he uses it all the time. Truthfully, he carries it everywhere in the pocket of his denim overalls, but he rarely needs it. Mr. Edwards is proud it has three settings: low, bright, and blinking. "I am thrilled about this flashlight, and I don't even need to buy batteries. All I have to do with this flashlight is plug it up every night." He kept the flashlight plugged in an outlet next to the sofa between the sofa and a tall *floor lamp.*

One day, Mr. Edwards was leaning and reaching to unplug his rechargeable flashlight. He was standing too far away, trying to avoid taking the extra steps to get closer. Reaching too far, he lost his balance and hit the floor. Sadly, he suffered a hip fracture, and his daughter moved in with him for several months to help with his care. Mr. Edwards enjoyed having her there, and she was happy that she was retired and available. They learned a lot about each other during that time – the good and not so good. She realized they were both stubborn. She was so happy to return to her house after he was better. He's now plugged his flashlight into an outlet on the backsplash of his kitchen counter, which is easy to reach.

Do you need to plan to ensure you do not overreach?

Can you see the benefits of eliminating the need to overreach for items? Can you see that your fall risks increase when you reach for things that are too far away? What changes can you make to relocate items so that you are not at risk of overreaching? Write it down so you don't forget.

FACT

75% of those aged 50+ would like to stay in their homes or communities for as long as possible.

(AARP, 2021)

TIP 11: AVOID USING STEP STOOLS AND LADDERS.

Why This Is Important:

Keep your feet on the floor. Moving items down to lower locations or using a reacher (a piece of adaptive equipment) can help you avoid the risks associated with climbing. Step stools, ladders, and even standing in a chair may seem like handy solutions for reaching high places, but this can be very dangerous. Your balance, strength, and coordination can decline as you age, making falls from even a small height more likely. Just know the floor will catch you if you fall – often resulting in serious injuries such as head injuries and fractures, particularly of the hip.

Real Life Story:

Betty, 74, has always loved to cook and spent hours preparing dishes from recipes handed down to her by her mother and grandmother. Her large home accommodated her huge family for all holidays and family functions. Everyone loved going to her house, especially for Thanksgiving dinner. Betty doesn't cook for large gatherings anymore, but she still has every type of pot, casserole dish, or cooking device you can imagine.

She loves that her children and grandchildren are continuing the family holiday gatherings. Her niece called to borrow a roasting pan. Betty loves to loan out things to her family; it makes her feel like she is contributing and helping. Betty rushed, wanting to retrieve the roasting pan from a top shelf in her pantry, wash it, and have it ready when her niece arrived. Betty was already reminiscing about the many times she had used the roasting pan, which her mother handed down; she imagined how delicious the turkey would taste, prepared using her grandmother's recipe.

Using a step stool to reach it, Betty grasped the sizeable roasting pan using both hands. Stepping down, she lost her balance and fell to the floor, where her niece found her. The family did gather for Thanksgiving, at her bedside as she was undergoing a series of tests to determine the extent of her injuries.

Do you need to plan not to use a step stool or ladder?

Can you see the benefits of avoiding the use of a step stool or ladder? Can you see that you are at an increased risk for falling when the step stool is unstable and when you are not holding onto a fixed sturdy surface for additional support? Yes, a step stool and ladder are for climbing to reach things, but are you safe to use them? What can you do differently? Who can you call to help? What items can be moved from high places? Think about it. Write down your thoughts while they are fresh in your mind.

TIP 12: INSTALL LEVER-STYLE DOOR KNOBS.

Why This Is Important:

Struggling to open a door with a round door knob can make it challenging to enter rooms and can result in loss of balance, leading to falls. Round door knobs are hard to grip and turn if your hands are weak or you have pain in your hands. You may think, "That's minor, I can tough it out." Why, when you don't have to? When you struggle to turn a door knob, you can cause arthritis in the hands to worsen. Also, when you lean your body in an effort to turn the knob, you can become off-balanced, increasing your risk of falling. Replacing turn-style door knobs with lever-style door knobs is an easy fix. The lever-style door knobs allow you to open a door by gently pushing a lever down, which enables the mechanism to move to allow the door to open.

Real-Life Story:

Ms. Claire hated her hands; she often put her hands behind her back whenever she had her picture taken. She blamed her "bad genes" for having arthritis in her hands. Her mother had it, and her grandmother had it too. Even as a little girl, she remembers how her mother's and grandmother's hands looked. She would often ask them why their fingers were not straight and why the knuckles on their fingers were so big. What she didn't realize was how painful their hands must have been because her fingers hurt a lot, especially when trying to turn a knob to open a door.

She often struggled and lost her balance as she attempted to turn the doorknob with both hands. She was always nervous about falling, so she didn't close many doors inside her home, often keeping them open or ajar. Opening her front and back doors was an ongoing struggle, but she thought it was just how life was for someone with arthritic hands.

One day when visiting her daughter's home, she noticed the lever-style door knob on the front entrance door. She saw how easy it was to open the door and mentioned it to her daughter. "I had them put on my doors because my hands were starting to hurt." Ms. Claire's heart sank, and she recommended that her 32-year-old daughter see a rheumatologist immediately, telling her not to make the mistake she had made, ignoring what was happening with her hands. Ms. Claire called and scheduled to have her doorknobs replaced; her daughter called and made a doctor's appointment.

Do you need to plan to switch to lever-style doorknobs on some of your doors?

Can you see the benefits of lever-style doorknobs? Can you see that this simple change can prevent a fall? Who can help you order and install them? Replacing doorknobs can be a low-cost fix, costing less than $50 for a doorknob. How many do you think you need? Write it down so you don't forget.

TIP 13: KEEP CORDS OUT OF WALKING PATHS.

Why This Is Important:

Extension and phone charger cords extending into your walking path are tripping hazards. You might think you know they're there—you see them every day and believe you can easily step over them. Many people thought the same, only to end up in the emergency room after a fall. Be honest— haven't you almost tripped on one already? It only takes one moment of distraction. Why continue to take a chance?

Real-Life Story:

Ms. Susan, 70, was fiercely independent, still driving, and with no significant health problems. She walked 2 miles almost daily, ate a reasonably healthy diet, and only took two medications. Ms. Susan had a small vegetable garden in her backyard, which she tended to every day. She prided herself on making healthy choices and vowed not to become a burden to her children, hoping she could stay in her home as long as possible. Her children often bragged that their mother was in better shape than they were.

One day, she had a scare. She usually charged her cell phone next to her bed but moved the cord to the den, so her phone could charge while she talked and folded laundry on the sofa. After finishing her folding, she was carrying a load of towels to the bathroom and forgot about the cord across the floor. Her foot became caught in the cord, but luckily, the cord pulled out of the wall. She's grateful she did not fall; it may have changed her life. Lesson learned.

Do you need to plan to keep cords and wires out of walking paths?

Can you see the benefits of keeping pathways in your home free of cords? Can you see that this simple change can prevent a fall? Are any cords needing to be rerouted away from your walking path? Make a note. Do it as soon as possible.

TIP 14: AVOID SITTING IN SEATS YOU STRUGGLE TO GET OUT OF.

Why This Is Important:

Struggling to get up from a worn-out, low, or sunken sofa or struggling to get out of a recliner or chair can lead to a fall. Standing can be challenging when a sofa is too low; this is especially true of old sofas with sunken cushions. Recliners can cause you to struggle because many swivel and rock, and the front end can go low to the floor, making standing challenging. Also, be aware that chairs with no armrests can cause you to struggle because you have nothing to help you push on to stand. These struggles result in a loss of balance, leading to falls. Many options are available to reduce the struggle and lower fall risks – armrest devices, risers, and replacing sofas and chairs are just a few. An occupational therapist can help determine the best option for you.

Real-Life Story:

It was a plaid, brown, peanut-butter, and cream-colored floral sofa with a ruffle skirt around the bottom, placed by a window that looked out onto the front yard. Over the years, the sofa, with paneled walls behind it, appeared in countless family photos, always in the same spot.

The cushions had long since sunken in, and throw pillows had been placed on top to make it taller and slightly easier for Deacon Jones to stand. Still, he struggled, and standing took him three to four trials. It wasn't that he loved the sofa; he just never thought about replacing it; he felt it had a lot of life still left in it.

Deacon Jones always sat on the sofa's right corner, looking out the window. He enjoyed watching cars go by, frequently muttering, 'There goes Alice,' or 'Where's Leroy headed now?' as he recognized the neighbors' cars. Recently, Deacon Jones started feeling pain in his right shoulder, which resulted from constantly pushing on the armrest to stand up. He began sitting longer each day, knowing it would hurt to stand. His leg muscles were weakening from inactivity. He hadn't fallen yet, but it was clear — it was time for a change in seating before it led to something worse."

His son came to visit from out of town and joined his dad on the sofa. He said that he felt like he "was sitting down into a bottomless pit" and his son struggled to get up. "Pops, you need a new sofa; this is bad," he said. After thinking about it, Deacon Jones agreed and purchased a new sofa, placing it in the same spot and looking out into the front yard.

Do you need a plan to avoid struggling to stand from a seat?

How mindful are you of where you sit? What seats are difficult for you to get up from? What changes can you make? Make a note.

TIP 15: USE PROPER TUB EQUIPMENT.

Why This Is Important:

When did you last get down in that tub and almost got stuck? It probably scared you half to death! Or how about when your leg got caught stepping in or out of the tub? You thought it was over! These are warning signs that you need a safer bathing plan. Tub seats and tub benches provide a secure seat for showering, and some eliminate the need to step over the tub's edge. Pairing these with other safety equipment can drastically reduce fall risks. Don't wait for another close call—invest in safety now to make your bathing experience safe and private.

Real-Life Story:

"I don't like showers. I didn't like them as a young girl, and I don't plan to start sitting on a seat and showering now. I enjoy getting in my tub and taking long hot baths to soak my achy legs and sore back in Epsom water. Plus, I don't feel clean unless I take a bath," Ms. Jean, 70, would say this whenever her daughter suggested using a tub bench and a hand-held shower head instead of sitting in the tub.

Ms. Jean was very private, always locking the bathroom door. Her daughter suspected Ms. Jean was struggling inside the bathroom, although she had not observed her. While Ms. Jean had never fallen, she admitted to some close calls. One day, Ms. Jean called out to her daughter; she could not get out of the tub; she couldn't do it. Ms. Jean now wished she had listened to her daughter. "I am so embarrassed! Having my grandson help me out of the tub is humiliating." Now, she has a tub bench and uses a hand-held shower, realizing that using the hand-held showerhead feels like heaven on her back. Her 22-year-old grandson is also relieved—he couldn't unsee what he saw!"

Do you need to plan not to fall or get stuck in the bathtub?

Can you see the benefits of using a tub seat, reducing the risks of falling or getting stuck in the tub? Various types of tub seats and tub benches are available. They are often paired with handheld showerheads and grab bars, with costs ranging from $25 to $200. Whole bathroom modifications are also an option and can carry a high ticket price. Is it time to rethink your bathing routine? An occupational therapist can help. You can talk with your doctor about it. Who can help you with this?

FACT

Falls are the leading cause of injury for adults ages 65 and over. Over 14 million or 1 in 4 older adults report falling every year.

(Centers for Disease Control and Prevention, 2024)

TIP 16: KEEP FLOORS DRY AND CLEAN SPILLS IMMEDIATELY.

Why This Is Important:

Wet floors can turn your floors into skating rinks, minus the fun. Be careful if you spill water or have a moment of incontinence because you cannot reach the bathroom on time. Slipping on a wet floor accounts for many falls in the home. If your floor becomes wet, safely clean it immediately or avoid that area until someone can help. If you clean it up yourself, you can sit in a chair next to a spill and wipe it up; don't lean over when standing, as you risk falling. Better yet, use a mop. Additionally, talk with a urologist or a pelvic floor therapist who can address issues with incontinence. Keeping floors dry prevents slips and falls, making your home safer.

Real-Life Story:

Incontinence is a taboo subject for many, but it shouldn't be. Often, people are afraid to discuss it or mistakenly believe it's inevitable with age. I worked with a client recovering from shoulder replacement surgery after a fall in her home.

Initially, she claimed the fall was due to dizziness, as mentioned in her discharge papers. However, after building rapport, she confided that the fall resulted from an incontinence episode—she had slipped on a wet spot in her bathroom. I encouraged her to use incontinence products, talk to her doctor, schedule a urologist appointment, and consult a pelvic floor therapist. Many are unaware that pelvic floor therapy, offered by occupational or physical therapists, can help manage incontinence. In her case, it was a preventable fall.

Do you need to plan to help keep your floors dry or to clean up spills?

Can you see the benefits of keeping your floors dry and spills-free? Can you see the importance of having a safe plan to clean up spills? Who can you call to help you? Plan to avoid a wet floor area if you do not have help. What can you do to manage incontinence? Make a note.

TIP 17: USE YOUR WALKING DEVICE.

Why This Is Important:

If your therapist has recommended using a cane or walker, following that advice is essential. These mobility aids significantly reduce fall risks. Holding onto walls and furniture may feel more natural, but it doesn't help when crossing open spaces. A cane or walker promotes better posture, making you stand upright and appear more youthful while ensuring your safety. With so many stylish options, including walkers with seats, there's no reason not to try one.

Real-Life Story:

Ms. Kathy has balance problems due to what she calls a"tee-ni-chy" (small, minute) stroke three years ago. Her physical therapist recommended that she use a walker to help with balance; Ms. Kathy, however, refuses. Ms. Kathy attends church religiously and loves receiving compliments from others, especially the newly appointed young pastor, who frequently comments that Ms. Kathy is always so "put together" in how she looks and dresses. She loves hearing that.

Ms Kathy would rather die than walk into church with a walker. "No way I'm going to let my friends see me using that thing," she tells herself. To appease her daughter, she began using a cane and is sure to say to her friends that she only used it to keep her daughter "off her back." The cane helps a little but does not provide the needed support; she is still unsteady. Ms. Kathy makes sure she gets to church early, walking in with a cane while holding onto a pew until she sits. She has started to park her car closer to the door and allows one of her "gentlemen friends" to help her to her car. She is a fall waiting to happen. Her daughter is concerned and keeps her mom on the prayer list.

Do you need to plan today to start using your walking device to help prevent a fall?

Can you see the benefits of using the walking device that your therapist has recommended? Do you have a device tucked away in a closet that you can use? Do you feel that you can honestly benefit from a walking device? Purchasing one online or at the corner drug store is one option. Still, the best thing to do is to be evaluated by a physical therapist to determine the device appropriate for you and to ensure that it is adjusted to the correct height. You can contact your doctor for an order for physical therapy and arrange for one visit to a local therapy clinic if that is all you need. Who can you call to help you to do this? Make a note.

TIP 18: REMOVE OR SECURE LOOSE CARPET.

Why This Is Important:

Carpet, when initially installed, is tight, and it creates a soft cushion under your feet as you walk. But over time, carpet can become loose and "bunchy" and look like waves of water. Be aware that loose carpet is a common trip hazard. It creates traps for your feet that can lead to falls. Even if you think you can simply avoid that spot on the carpet, be careful, especially when it is in your direct walking path. It only takes one moment of distraction to cause your feet to become caught in the loose carpeting, and down you go. Serious injuries, such as fractures or head trauma, can occur. By securing or removing loose carpet, you can create a safer environment. Don't underestimate the danger—address it now to prevent a potential accident.

Real-Life Story:

Mr. Calvin, a widower, built his home; he and his brothers hung each piece of lumber and nailed every board together. He was so proud of the home he provided for his wife and that he could raise all their children there. Mr. Calvin secretly hoped that one day, one of his sons would move back to town and live in the home after he passed away; he would love to see it remain in the family. Mr. Calvin had only updated the house a little over the years. He knew the carpet was loose and would be careful not to step on it where it bunched up. He had planned to one day have the carpet smoothed back out but not replace it even though it had been in the house for nearly thirty years.

One day, when rushing to answer the door for a package delivery, Mr. Calvin's foot got caught in the carpet, and down he went—TIMBER! He did recover and eventually returned to his home after several weeks in rehab and a stay in a skilled nursing unit (located in a nursing home), where he saw some familiar faces that he grew up with. Being in the nursing home's skilled nursing unit for 35 days was quite an eye-opener for Mr. Calvin. He promised himself that he would update his house to prevent future falls. He allowed his sons to have the carpet replaced while he was in the skilled nursing unit and to make other needed changes before he returned home.

Do you need a plan to repair or remove loose carpet?

Can you see the benefits of securing down carpet that has loosened and bunched up or has a loose end? Do you know the danger of getting your foot caught under the edge of the carpet detached from the floor? Fixing this problem can be as simple as having the carpet stretched out and reattached. Better yet, is it time to see that old carpet go? Ignoring this is like waiting for a fall to happen. Who can help you with this? What are your thoughts? Write them down so you don't forget.

TIP 19: BE AWARE OF PETS AND HOW YOU CARE FOR THEM.

Why This Is Important:

Pets are adorable and make excellent companions, but they can also be or leave obstacles on the floor that cause a fall. Yes, they are cute, and you think you can read their minds, but be careful.

Leaning down to pick up pets or weaving around the many balls, bones, stuffed animals, and squeaky toys can cause you to lose your balance, particularly if you have mobility issues. Picking up a pet bowl from the floor to fill or empty can also be hazardous; you might find yourself on the floor next to your pet.

To prevent falls, keep pet areas organized, train pets to stay clear of your feet when walking, and have a safe way of providing them food and water. Taking precautions helps ensure both your safety and the well-being of your pet.

Real-Life Story:

> *Your beloved pet may be the most intelligent animal on earth, but it can't call 911 if you fall. Be careful. Such was the case with Ms. Jen; she stepped on a tennis ball (one of the many) belonging to Red, her golden retriever. She fell and sustained a hip fracture. She lay on the floor for hours as Red brought her all of his squeaky toys and snuggled next to her. Ms. Jen's brother found her there. She underwent hip surgery but then refused to participate in in-patient rehab after her surgery. Against the orthopedic surgeon's recommendation and her family's recommendation, she insisted on going*

home immediately because she couldn't bear to think of Red sleeping on the floor at her brother's house. Her brother was adamant, "I like Red, but he's not sleeping in the bed with me. I'm already gonna have a hard time dealing with all the hair he drops everywhere, and I'm not gonna be able to eat in peace."

Her returning home immediately was hard on the entire family. She received physical and occupational therapy at home, and a caregiver had to be hired to help with her care and to keep Red out of the way.

Do you need a plan that helps you to care for your pet safely?

Can you see the benefits of keeping your pet and its toys away from your feet as you walk in your home? Do you find it difficult to fill or empty their food bowls safely? Now is the time to do something about it. Take this seriously; your dog needs you to be healthy. This tip is potentially a no-cost fix. Who can help you with this? What are your thoughts on how you can reduce this fall risk? Write them down so you don't forget.

TIP 20: AVOID WEARING LONG CLOTHING THAT DRAGS ON THE FLOOR.

Why This Is Important:

Extra long dresses and pants can cause your feet to become entangled or create a slippery surface under your feet. You may have unintentionally purchased them this way, or it can occur if you have recently lost weight. When your clothing drags on the floor, it increases your risk of falling. Pants with cumbersome fasteners can also potentially result in a tripping hazard due to the fasteners remaining open and causing the pants to slide down. Ensure your clothes fit properly and are easy to manage. Consider having clothes altered or ordering adaptive clothing apparel online that is designed stylishly and allows you to be safe and maintain your dignity.

Real-Life Story:

Mr. Stephen, 80, was a retired businessman. He wore khakis with a belt and a tucked-in dress shirt to work for 60 years. Now retired and experiencing weakness and hip pain, Mr. Stephen struggles with daily tasks. In the bathroom, he unfastens his belt and pants and sits for toileting. After toileting, he struggles to keep his balance while pulling up his pants. He also becomes tired when working with the zipper and belt and often leaves them unfastened.

Mr. Stephen recently fell when his pants slid down to his ankles, sustaining minor injuries. He was now afraid he would have to move out of his home.

His daughter stepped in to help and recommended he switch to khakis with elastic waistbands that are easy to pull up. She also had grab bars installed near the toilet. Mr. Stephen, to his surprise, is proud of his new look and is grateful that he can continue to live in his home alone. His daughter checks on him every couple of days. He is thankful for his daughter's support and is now more accepting of change. This fall was preventable.

Do you need a plan that prevents the wearing of long clothing that drags on the floor? Or fasteners that are difficult to manage?

Can you see the benefits of avoiding wearing clothing that is too long? Can you see that it is easy to trip on the excess fabric that can wrap under your feet? Can you see the hazards of having fasteners that are difficult to manage? Having your dresses/pants hemmed or altered or switching to elastic waistbands on your pants are simple solutions. Shopping for new clothes that fit is also an exciting option. Who can help you with this? Who do you know that sews? Are you willing to go shopping for new clothes that fit or order online? Think about it. Write down your thoughts. Don't wait.

FACT

More fall-related emergency room visits were due to falls at home (79.2%) compared to falls not at home (20.8%).

(American Journal of Lifestyle Medicine, 2020)

TIP 21: AVOID BENDING TO PICK UP ITEMS OFF THE FLOOR.

Why This Is Important:

Bending over to pick up items from the floor while standing puts you at risk for a fall, especially if you have mobility or balance issues. Using assistive devices such as a reacher (sometimes called a grabber) extends your arm's length and reach, allowing you to pick up things off the floor with minimal bending of your hips. A reacher also comes in hand to pick up a newspaper lying in your driveway and can even help you put on pants. This inexpensive device can save you from losing your balance and landing on the floor.

Real-Life Story:

Josephine, 78, knew in her heart that living alone in her home may soon end. She hated relying on her son for so much support and tried hard not to bother him. Everyday tasks were becoming increasingly difficult to manage, but Josephine was determined to give her best effort, saying she would not give up without a fight. She has balance problems due to her chronic dizziness, which started after a car accident several years ago. Josephine owns a reacher, kept in her laundry room and used to help her get her clothes out of the dryer.

One day, she dropped her last pink packet of artificial sweetener in the kitchen on the floor. Josephine knew bending over to pick it up was risky because she had previously done this and had fallen. But this day, she didn't feel she had the energy to walk to the laundry room to retrieve the reacher. She wanted to finish making her tea so that she could sit to watch a rerun of

"Match Game."

She decided to bend over to pick it up with her hand. She leaned down to get the pink packet, then stopped. "I must be losing my mind; what am I thinking? Gene Rayburn, Betty White, and Nipsy Russell can wait; they are all dead anyway." She got the reacher; it took her 3-4 times to grab it with the reacher, but she got it. She made it to her recliner, sat catching her breath while drinking her tea, and laughed as she watched a rerun of "Hollywood Squares." "Phyliss Diller cracks me up," she said. Fall averted.

Do you need a plan that prevents you from bending over to pick up things off the floor?

Can you see the benefits of not bending over while standing to pick up an item off the floor? Some people are safe to do this, but some are not, especially those with balance problems. Also, when that item is tiny, you must have fine motor precision to pick it up.

Leaving things on the floor until you get help is allowed; just make sure you move it out of the path you walk in. Sitting on a chair to pick up the item is also an option. Also, consider investing in a reacher or two; you can get them online and at most stores for less than $20. They come in handy for lots of things. Changing your behavior is the biggest cost to you. Are you willing to order that reacher? What are your thoughts? Write them down so you don't forget.

TIP 22: AVOID RUSHING TO ANSWER THE PHONE OR DOOR.

Why This Is Important:

Rushing can lead to accidents, especially if you're not paying attention to your surroundings. Slow down. Don't rush to the phone; carry a cell or cordless phone. Keep the phone in your pocket or have a safe way to take it as you move around your home. Chances are it's just a spam call anyway —you don't have any student loans, and your car warranty isn't expiring. Installing a video doorbell can allow you to see and talk to someone at your door. Nothing is so important that you rush, lose your balance, or trip on something. If the call or visitor needs to speak with you, they will wait or call back. Your safety should always come first.

Real-Life Story:

Ms. Jessie Mae, 65, has severe arthritis and knee pain. She is also overweight and uses a walker. She is hoping to have knee replacement surgery soon so she can get her life back, but her doctor wants her to lose at least 60 lbs first. She's been eating more healthily and has already lost 43 lbs. Ms. Jessie Mae is proud of her progress but was discouraged because she hit a plateau in her weight loss, so she ordered several weight-loss shakes. She has been waiting 5-7 business days to receive her packages and just received the notification on her phone that her packages were left at her front door.

Eager to get her packages so she could make one of the banana sundae milkshakes, Ms. Jessie Mae rushed to the front door. Not watching what she was doing, the leg of her walker became caught on the door molding in her dining room, and down she went to the floor.

Thankfully, Ms. Jessie Mae wasn't injured but couldn't get off the floor alone. She could call the fire department, which arrived and helped her get off the floor. One of the handsome young firemen brought her packages into the house for her. Ms. Jessie Mae was sore the next day and loved the banana sundae flavor, the pecan praline flavor, and the double fudge flavor weight-loss shakes she had already tried. This fall was preventable.

Do you need a plan that prevents you from rushing to answer the door or phone?

Can you see the benefits of slowing down and not getting in a hurry? Can you see that a fall can happen in an instant when you are not paying attention to your surroundings? There are things that you can determine to do instead of rushing. Consider the doorbell camera, keep your phone handy, or be okay with calling someone back if you miss their call. What are your thoughts? What can you change about your behavior? Write it down so you don't forget.

TIP 23: HAVE THE CORRECT BED HEIGHT.

Why This Is Important:

When your bed is the correct height, getting in and out of it requires less effort. A bed that is too tall can make it challenging to get in and unsafe to sit on the side, potentially causing you to slide off onto the floor. Conversely, a bed that is too low can make standing up difficult when sitting on the edge. Many aging adults resort to using a step stool or crawling into a tall bed on their hands and knees like ninjas, which is not always safe. Adjusting your bed to the appropriate height ensures your feet can rest flat on the floor when sitting on the side of the bed, thus reducing fall risks. An occupational therapist can help determine the appropriate height and options, which can include replacing your boxspring with a low-profile one, adding a bed rail, or switching to a hospital bed –depending on your needs, physical limitations, and budget.

Real-Life Story:

> *Mr. David, 55, has weakness due to MS (multiple sclerosis). He is divorced and lives alone. He manages okay for most things. He is an early riser, having worked as a warehouse foreman for years at a plant, clocking in at 4:15 am. He feels stir-crazy when he has to lie awake until 7am when his daughter can help him because he can not safely get out of bed alone. He has fallen several times in the past, sustaining several minor injuries.*
>
> *His daughter lives "sort of close by" and has to come over every morning*

to help him out of bed because he can not afford a caregiver. It is a hectic morning for the daughter because she has to go to her dad's house before taking her son to school first (because if she didn't, he would try to get up on his own). Helping her dad often prevents her from getting her son into the elementary school carpool line on time. She always feels rushed and hates getting her one-year-old in and out of the car seat to check-in her 5-year-old son at school when they arrive after the tardy bell rings.

Both Mr. David and his daughter needed a change. She called his doctor, tearful. The nurse sent her a list of community resources. Mr. David qualified for home health services, and I became his occupational therapist. I recommended lowering his bed by switching to a low-profile box spring (4" tall) and adding a bed rail. It dropped the bed by 6 inches. I also recommended that he learn to adapt his behaviors, which would reduce his daughter's stress. With training, Mr. David learned to get in and out of bed independently and perform personal tasks with improved independence. Things were better, and there were no more falls for now.

Do you need a plan to ensure that your bed is at the proper height?

Can you see the benefits of having a bed height raised or lowered? There are many options available to achieve this goal. A mobile private practice or home health occupational therapist can help you determine and achieve the appropriate height needed for your bed. What are your thoughts? Write it down.

TIP 24: HAVE YOUR VISION CHECKED REGULARLY.

Why This Is Important:

Can you really see what you need to see? For some, you just get used to "seeing the way you see" and don't realize how much of life you are missing and how much you are struggling. Impaired vision can lead to falls. If your doctor has mentioned that you have a vision problem but you don't remember the name of the specific diagnosis, all you know is, " It had a funny name," you need to go in to see them. Learn the name of the vision disorder and how your vision is affected by that disease.

If things look cloudy, or you cannot see the entire room, you could have something serious happening. Are you bumping into furniture? Are you looking for something that you know should be right in front of you? That's scary—you could trip and fall. How can you change your environment and behavior to compensate for visual losses? Regular vision check-ups are essential in fall prevention.

Real-Life Story:

Mr. Joe, 71, had cataracts, which the ophthalmologist had mentioned to him last year. Mr. Joe is married and retired. He doesn't allow his wife to go to doctor's appointments with him; he thinks she talks too much and asks too many questions.

His son noticed that his dad's movements were slow and unsteady, and his wife also noticed that Mr. Joe had bruises on his left shoulder and a knot on his left leg. After pressuring him repeatedly, Mr. Joe reluctantly admitted to his wife that he had tripped over the leg of a table and fallen a couple of days earlier; he didn't see the table and wondered if his wife had moved the table when she was cleaning.

The son convinced his dad to schedule an eye exam, and Mr. Joe allowed his son to go with him, his son learned that his father had cataracts. The ophthalmologist provided education and brochures on cataracts to Mr. Joe and his son. He explained that the removal of cataracts would result in improved vision. Mr. Joe and his son were glad to learn this, and the surgery was scheduled for the following week. "If he wasn't trying to be so private and wasn't so hardheaded, he could have already had that surgery. I know about cataracts; I could have told him he needed to have it done," his wife stated.

Do you need a plan to have your vision checked regularly?

Can you see the benefits of having your eyes checked regularly? Can you see that it is essential to know what is wrong with your eyes and that all eye disorders are different? Have you had your eyes checked recently? Do you wear your glasses as you should? Do you know the name of the eye doctor that you see? Can you find their phone number? Do you like them? Do you need to change to someone whose office is closer? Think about it. Who can help you? What are your thoughts? What do you plan to do? Write it down so you don't forget.

TIP 25: WEAR YOUR HEARING AIDS.

Why This Is Important:

Decreased hearing affects your ability to detect sounds that can alert you to dangers in your home, such as alarms, doorbells, or even someone calling your name. Decreased hearing can increase the risk of accidents and falls. Also, when you can not hear properly, you might misjudge distances or miss auditory cues that help balance and navigation. Hearing aids can significantly improve your safety and overall quality of life. Many resist getting hearing aids. Some don't think they need them, some don't believe they can afford them, and others buy the hearing aids but don't wear them. Why pay for those hearing aids and not want to wear them?

Real-Life Story:

Mr. Billy's wife stated, "He never wants to wear his hearing aids, and it bugs me. We paid all that money for them, and now he says that he doesn't like how they sound and can't hear clearly with them in. The hearing aid place told us that it might take a couple of adjustments to get it right; we went back once, and it didn't help much, so he said he wasn't going back; that was nine months ago.

" After recently having bloodwork done, Mr. Billy's doctor's office nurse called and informed his wife of a change in his blood pressure medication. Mr. Billy did not hear the phone ringing as he watched television with a 90 out of 100 volume. The wife relayed the message to Mr. Billy, instructing him to cut his blood pressure medication in half, now taking half a pill twice a day. As always, Mr. Billy replied, "Okay," knowing he did not understand

what his wife said. Mr. Billy doubled his medication dosage, taking two pills twice a day for three days. He became dizzy and had a fall.

A trip to the emergency room revealed Mr. Billy had a blood pressure reading of 70/50. Upon review of his medications, it was discovered Mr. Billy had made an error. His wife was annoyed, stating, "He knew he didn't hear me but knows I get so tired of him saying 'Whatcha say?' so he never lets me know that he doesn't hear me." His wife made a follow-up appointment with the audiologist. The audiologist wondered why Mr. Billy hadn't returned sooner. Within minutes, he was hearing clearly. Mr. Billy could now hear and understand what "he wanted to hear."

Do you need a plan to have your hearing checked regularly?

Can you see the benefits of having your hearing checked regularly? If you constantly ask people to repeat what they have said or knowingly pretend to understand what someone has said, you are putting yourself at risk. If your hearing aids are no longer working correctly, are broken or lost, or if the dog has eaten them, it is time to look at replacing them. Check with your insurance; they may pay for a portion of them. Who can help you with this? What are your thoughts? What do you plan to do? Write it down so you don't forget.

FACT

In 2019, 83% of hip fracture deaths and 88%
of emergency department visits

and hospitalizations for hip fractures were caused by falls.

(Journal On Aging and Health, 2023)

TIP 26: STAY ACTIVE AND KEEP MOVING.

Why This Is Important:

You have to keep moving! It's called getting some exercise. Don't over-complicate it. I'm not suggesting you sign up for a 5k run or gym membership. Get your doctor's okay, then just get up and move around. Do things that cause your arms and legs to move and increase your heart rate. Begin by walking inside the house. Try standing up and marching in place during the commercials of your favorite television shows. You can even sit and do exercises. Make it fun, and see if you can find a friend to be accountable to or join in with you. Talk with your doctor to see if it's okay to start walking up and down your driveway or even participate in a dance class a couple of days a week. Exercise is good for your joints, muscles, heart, and brain. Exercising keeps you strong, improves your balance, and can prevent you from having falls.

Real-Life Story:

Once you retire, you want to relax. "You've earned it, right?" That is what Ms. Cassie thought, and she was enjoying her retirement. She loved her courtroom shows, especially Judge Judy, even though she thought she was mean and arrogant. Ms. Cassie was also secretly addicted to "that awful show that helped those girls find out who the baby's daddy is" but kept it a secret from her children. Her activity level dwindled from working five days a week at a local bakery to just walking from the bedroom to the kitchen, to the den, to the bathroom, and a lot of sitting.

A year into retirement, she started to feel weak and mentioned to her doctor that she was having some new hip and knee pain, that she felt unsteady, and had nearly fallen a couple of times. Bloodwork and a cardiac workup by a cardiologist revealed no serious problems. A review of her activity level revealed that she had become a "couch potato." The doctor recommended that she add exercises and restructure her day to include loops of walking inside her house from the den, through the unused dining room, "use-to-be-formal living room," then through her kitchen, and back to her chair in the den.

Ms. Cassie honestly thought that moving would cause her hips and knees to hurt more, but she gave it a try. Surprisingly, Ms. Cassie soon stopped having joint pain and felt stronger. She even managed to wean herself off some of those corrupted shows of our justice system.

Do you need a plan that allows you to add exercise and movement into your day?

Can you see the benefits of adding exercise and movement into your day? Do you realize that you can lose muscle mass and strength, and it leads to falls? But guess what? You can start to turn things around today. First, talk to your doctor; if he has already told you to start exercising, then you don't need to ask; just begin. Commit to 15 minutes a day, then gradually increase it. What exercises can you add in? Think about what you can do. Who can motivate you to commit to it? Write it down right now so you don't forget or change your mind.

TIP 27: WEAR ENCLOSED SHOES THAT FIT PROPERLY.

Why This Is Important:

Your footwear significantly affects your feet's interaction with the environment and the information they provide to your body for balance. Shoes without an enclosed heel alter your biomechanics and posture. An altered walking pattern increases the risk of tripping. You don't need to wear steel-toe boots, but your heel should be inside a shoe; this automatically eliminates flip-flops and specific house slippers. "Flip-flops" include shoes that are too small, causing you to walk on the back of the shoe, and shoes that are too big, which cause your foot to move up and down inside the shoe; both can increase your fall risks. Improper shoes contribute to many falls.

Real-Life Story:

Ms. B, a widow, received a pair of gold house slippers from her son, her now only son, due to the loss of her younger son a year ago. The slippers were metallic gold with a small wedge sole, just like a pair she had in the 80s. Her son usually was not a thoughtful gift-giver, so she was delighted that he gave her a gift for her birthday that she would use. The sparkly slippers, however, had an open heel and were too narrow. Ms. B's feet didn't go all the way into the slippers, and her heels extended off the back, but she didn't want to tell her son they didn't fit. When he visited, she wore them and could tell he was proud that she loved his gift. Everything was okay as long as she was concentrating and walking in a straight line. Ms. B could tolerate wearing them and "act normal."

But one day, while making their favorite lunch, a grilled cheese sandwich and tomato soup, she turned around to open the refrigerator and went down onto the hard tile floor. The slippers had stayed in place, but her feet pivoted out of them, causing her to fall. Ms. B sustained a left foot fracture but did not require surgery. She was non-weight bearing on her foot for six weeks and had to wear a heavy walking boot on her foot and use a crutch. It took five months and physical therapy to recover fully.

After that, her son insisted that she no longer wear the slippers. Ms. B never wore them again but occasionally took them out of the box and looked at them. The golden slippers brought back many fond memories of her husband and the time she spent with her boys years and years ago. She treasured her gift. This fall was preventable.

Do you need a plan that allows you to only wear properly fitting, enclosed shoes?

Do you see that it is essential to wear properly fitting shoes that do not have heels out? Do you see how fast a fall can occur? It is time to retire shoes with the heel out, that are too little, or are too big. Ensure you have comfortable enclosed shoes at home and for wear when attending functions. If your feet tend to swell, make sure you have shoes of different sizes available, shoes that can be adjusted to fit your foot or wear properly fitting non-skid socks if needed. Who can help you with this? Write it down right now so you don't forget.

TIP 28: KNOW THE SIDE EFFECTS OF YOUR MEDICATIONS.

Why This Is Important:

Some medications come with adverse side effects, including dizziness and drowsiness. It's crucial to note how you feel after starting a new medication. Report any dizziness or drowsiness to your doctor. Additionally, inform your primary care doctor about all the medicines you're taking, including those from another medical specialist, over-the-counter vitamins, and any new miracle "all-natural" cure pills recommended by friends or family. Some of those "all-natural" pills may negatively react with your prescribed medications and cause lightheadedness or make you start seeing weird things on the wall, which can make you run, trip, and fall! Think about it: what medical degree does your church friend or sister-in-law have? How's their health anyway? Don't they have more problems, aches, and pains than you? Why are you listening to them?

Real-Life Story:

Ms. Kathy, 69, has a daughter whose co-worker claimed that her mother had more energy after starting a new organic vitamin that boosts the immune system and rids the body of toxins. Convinced by the weekly updates on the improvements, Ms. Kathy's daughter ordered the vitamin and persuaded Ms. Kathy to try it.

A week into taking the miracle pill, Ms. Kathy began feeling weak, nauseated, and lightheaded. Her balance was a little off, and she couldn't pinpoint why. Her daughter was glad the new organic miracle pill was already fortifying her. Otherwise, things may be much worse. She also recommended that mom now take two vitamins a day to help increase her strength and speedily begin to feel better. A week later, Ms. Kathy had a fall. She did not land on the floor but fell back onto the sofa after attempting to stand to go to the bathroom.

A visit to her doctor was scheduled, and blood work was performed, revealing lab abnormalities. After casually mentioning the all-natural, organic, miracle vitamin her daughter recommended she take, her doctor instructed her to stop taking it immediately. Thankfully, after repeating her labs ten days later, all her blood levels had returned to normal. Ms. Kathy recovered. She was back to doing everything she had previously done –A miracle. Know what you are putting in your mouth!

Do you need a plan that ensures that you always check the side effects of all your medications?

Do you see that knowing the side effects of your medications is vital? Do you know that dizziness and drowsiness are side effects of many drugs and can lead to falls? Tell your doctor everything you are taking – including creams, vitamins, eye drops, mushrooms, everything! Don't believe everything you hear about miracle drugs. Please notify your doctor of any adverse side effects of your medications. Who can help you with this? Write it down right now so you don't forget.

TIP 29: FIND A MIDDLE GROUND WITH YOUR CHILDREN.

Why This Is Important:

Your children love you, and sometimes their concern can come across as bossiness, like they are trying to run and ruin your life. They may even pressure you to move out of your home because they see you are starting to have some struggles or are at risk for a fall. I advise you not to turn a deaf ear to all they say. Even if you don't like their tone, listen to their words. Be honest with yourself: Are they pointing out valid fall risks or overreacting? It's probably a combination of both. The truth is, they may not know the best solutions, but neither do you. Seek help from a professional. Find an occupational therapist specializing in fall prevention and a certified aging-in-place specialist. Don't just call a handyman, who doesn't know what's best for you. Be willing to improve your safety. After all, if you do fall and have a severe injury, it impacts your children's lives as well as yours.

Real-Life Story:

Ms. Anna's daughter is a real worry-wart, always concerned about her mom falling since her dad died and her mom decided to remain in their family home. After contracting COVID in 2021, Ms. Anna has residual weakness and tires quickly. Her movements are slow but relatively steady and she has never fallen.

Her daughter, however, noticed that Ms. Anna had stopped taking baths and now only "washed up" at the sink because she no longer felt safe and feared falling in the tub. Her daughter wants Ms. Anna to move into assisted living, but Ms. Anna is adamant about staying in her home. This disagreement has caused a lot of tension between them, and Ms. Anna dreads her daughter's visits because she always brings up the subject.

Her daughter voiced her concerns to Ms. Anna's doctor, and occupational therapy was ordered. Many fall risks were identified after the OT performed a home safety assessment. The OT recommended safety equipment, assisted with the setup, and provided training on the proper technique for safely performing everyday tasks. Ms. Anna was also trained in appropriate energy conservation and fall prevention strategies. Lastly, the OT recommended minor structural modifications requiring hiring a contractor or handyman.

Ms. Anna agreed to some of the changes and rejected some; it was a start. Both Ms. Anna and her daughter were amazed at how the changes significantly improved Ms. Anna's level of safety in the home, even allowing her to use her shower.

Do you need a plan that includes you seeking professional advice on home safety?

When you are cognitively able to, you should be allowed to make your own decisions about how you live in your home, but realize, you must be willing to live with the consequences of your choices. Please remain open-minded. If you are not open to listening to your adult children's recommendations, an occupational therapy evaluation is an option. Are you willing to contact your doctor? Who can help you with this? Write it down right now so you don't forget.

TIP 30: LISTEN TO YOUR GUT FEELING.

Why This Is Important

Often, your inner voice or gut feeling can be your best guide regarding safety. When properly functioning, this inner voice frequently draws from your past experiences, observations of others' mistakes, and basic common sense. It's like an internal alarm system warning of the potential for things to go wrong. Trusting these instincts can help you avoid potential hazards. Many get these warnings but dismiss them, thinking, "I'll just do it this way this one time; I'll be ok." Please listen—your body and mind naturally warn you about danger, shaped by years of learning and experiences. When warnings are heeded, falls are averted.

Real-Life Story

Ms. Patsy, 64, recently retired after working years as an English professor at the local community college. She had hoped to work one more year but threw in the towel early after a new Dean took over her department.

Ms. Patsy spends her days reading while sitting on her patio and enjoying her latest passion – bird watching. She had long read many books about hummingbirds and was becoming more fascinated by them. Ms. Patsy loved feeding them in her backyard and often sat for hours, watching them and laughing at how aggressive they could be. She named the bossy one "Bogart", the same name she secretly gave to her old boss. She laughed at Bogart and said, "There you go again, beating other birds down, trying to get everything for yourself."

She usually refilled the hummingbird feeder 3-4 times a week. Noticing that the feeder was empty, she headed outside to fill it. As she went outside, she thought, "Go get your call alert necklace; you always wear it when you go outside." Without a second thought, Ms. Patsy turned around, retrieved the necklace, and placed it around her neck.

When she stepped onto the dew-covered patio, it was like stepping onto a sheet of ice, and down she went, sustaining a wrist injury and unable to get up. She said, "I was so glad I had that necklace on. There is no telling how long I would have had to lay there watching Bogart carrying on like a lunatic, like I was lying there on purpose and not filling up the feeder."

Do you need to plan to be mindful of your gut feeling?

Do you understand that you have an internal warning system that can alert you of possible danger? Have you ever had an injury or accident that, in hindsight, could have been prevented if you had heeded the warning? Learn from your mistakes. Don't be your worst enemy. Listen to the warning. Think about it. When have you not heeded a warning? Write it down right now so you don't forget.

FACT

Home visits by occupational therapists can prevent falls
among older people who are at increased risk of falling.
However, the effect may not be caused by home modifications
alone. Home visits by occupational therapists may also lead
to changes in behavior that enable older people to live more
safely in both the home and the external environment.

(Cumming et al., 1999)

TIP 31: CONTINUE TO EDUCATE YOURSELF.

Why This Is Important

Continuing to educate yourself about fall risks and fall prevention is essential. Don't think that you know it all; nobody does. Stay up-to-date on new safety devices, home modification techniques, and health-related information. Learn what changes to make in your home and how to adjust your activities after an illness or new diagnosis. Take advantage of community workshops and online courses focused on fall prevention and improving your ability to remain safe at home. Education empowers you to make informed decisions, spot potential hazards, and proactively avoid accidents. It also helps you stay engaged and mentally sharp, improving your quality of life. You are never too old to learn something new.

Real-Life Story

Mr. Tom, 78, lives alone and loves keeping life simple. He has always been skeptical about technology, never owning a computer, but he finally agreed to use a cell phone—a flip phone. His son is always concerned about his father's safety, especially since his father's neighborhood is not as safe as it used to be.

After much persuasion, Mr. Tom hesitantly agreed to install internet services at his home so his son could install a doorbell camera and other outdoor cameras around his house. Mr. Tom soon appreciated these safety features and admitted that he feels safer knowing that his son watches things outside his home through his smartphone. Mr. Tom is now amazed at the advances in technology, "I can't believe all the things that a little phone can do now," he stated.

Mr. Tom later received a smart tablet from his grandson, who lives out of state. His grandson programmed his out-of-state phone number and put the new baby's pictures on the tablet. Mr. Tom now enjoys video-calling his grandson and getting to know his great-grandson. Life is no longer so lonely for Mr. Tom. He's proud to remain in his home alone and still feel close and connected to his family.

Do you need a plan to ensure that you continue to educate yourself?

Can you see the benefits of being a continued learner? Do you know that you are not too old to learn new things? I want to challenge you to remain open-minded. Be willing to make changes that will allow you to increase your level of safety in your home and increase your socialization with others. Consider taking an online class or group that meets weekly. Be willing to try new things; you may just like them. What events are happening in your community? Who can help you connect with organizations? Do you have transportation to events? Who can help with this? What are your thoughts? Who can help you? Write it down.

YOU'VE MADE IT TO THE END! CONGRATULATIONS.

Thank you for investing your time in reading this book. I hope it has inspired you to take actionable steps toward reducing your fall risks and living more safely and independently.

Many of the recommendations that can make a significant difference are simple yet highly effective. Best of all, many of them can be done without hiring a professional or spending a lot of money. However, there are some recommended changes that are more complex, especially if you have specific needs related to a diagnosis or disability. In these cases, I strongly recommend seeking the expertise of an Occupational Therapist to ensure that your space is tailored to your unique situation.

EQUIPMENT RECOMMENDATIONS:

There are two classifications of equipment:

Adaptive equipment (AE) refers to tools or devices that help make daily activities more accessible, like grab bars, reachers, doorknobs, sock-aids, adaptive spoons, etc. These items can improve safety and independence but aren't always considered medical necessities.

Durable medical equipment (DME) includes medically necessary items like bedside commodes, walkers, wheelchairs, hospital beds, and oxygen equipment used long-term for managing a health condition.

Medicare does not cover adaptive equipment because it's not deemed medically necessary. However, Medicare will pay for specific durable medical equipment if you have a qualified diagnosis that proves you need it and your doctor writes an order supporting that need.

I'm including a list of equipment mentioned in this book. All of these devices can be obtained online or at a local store. These are devices that I have recommended and used often.

Please note that the exact equipment you may need may differ from my recommendation. It is recommended that an occupational therapist is consulted to determine the individual's specific limitations and needs.

Tip 1: Grab bars: Wall mounted; Avoid suction-mounted grab bars.

Tip 2: Non-skid mat for tub/shower: one for inside tub/shower and one for temporary use on the floor outside shower/tub.

Tip 3: Toilet riser with armrests, which locks in place; Bedside commode frame over toilet; You can also opt to add armrests only, but it is best not to get armrests with legs that rest on the floor.

Tip 4: LED light Bulbs

Tip 8: Motion sensor night light

Tip 9: Non-skid socks

Tip 12: Lever-style doorknobs

Tip 15: Tub bench or Tub seat; Handheld Showerhead; Grab bars (Note: Tub bench is best if unable to step over into a tub)

Tip 21: Reacher: Lightweight one for indoor; heavy-duty one with suction tips for outside use.

Tip 22: Doorbell Camera

Tip 23: Low Profile Boxspring; Bedrail. (Low profile boxsprings come in several heights and replace standard height boxsprings, causing bed to be lower. When choosing a bed rail, look for a narrow one or one with a bag that occludes the opening and prevents a head from entering inside the bedrail.)

Tip 27: Enclosed rubber sole shoes

Tip 30: Call-Alert necklace or bracelet.

Visit my website, Findingafoothold.com, for direct links to the products above.

FALL PREVENTION ACTION LIST: WHAT ARE YOU PLANNING TO DO?

Tip #:   Plan:

_____

_____

_____

_____

_____

_____

_____

_____

_____

_____

_____

_____

_____

_____

_____

_____

_____

_____

Tip #:   Plan:

_____

_____

_____

CONCLUSION

It's easy to think, "I won't fall; I know how to be careful." However, many older adults are unaware of the hazards in their homes, risky behaviors they engage in, or the changes in their bodies that naturally occur with aging. These factors can make them more vulnerable to falls than they realize.

The stories in this book are real experiences of patients and families I've had the honor to meet—none of whom expected a fall to happen to them. The truth is, no one wakes up thinking, "I'm going to fall today," but then is in disbelief to find their life has changed after sustaining an injury.

Be encouraged. I want you to know that you don't have to fall. You can take simple, practical steps today to significantly reduce your risk. Start with the tips in this book as a baseline of where to start, and discuss any concerns with your family.

Many recommendations are easy to implement, while others may require guidance from an occupational therapist (OT) or physical therapist (PT). Your doctor can help by providing a referral for a home health or private practice OT or PT who can assess your home, help tailor modifications to your needs and development a strength and balance program for you to follow.

Remember, while making environmental changes is essential, changing behaviors is just as critical in preventing falls. Millions of older adults successfully age in place, and with careful planning and a willingness to make adjustments, you can, too.

I invite you to take the National Council on Aging "Falls Free CheckUp" to learn more about your fall risks. Answer 13 simple questions to get your fall risk score and resources to prevent falls.

As part of this journey, I also invite you to visit the CDC's (Center for Disease Control) website: https://www.cdc.gov/steadi/index.html for more information on fall prevention. STEADI = (Stop Elderly Accidents, Deaths & Injuries).

ABOUT THE AUTHOR

Consuela R Marshall

Consuela Marshall is an Occupational Therapist, Certified Aging In Place Specialist, Fall Prevention Specialist, Certified Dementia Practioner, and Certified Geriatric Care Professional. With nearly 30 years of experience and having entered thousands of homes, she has witnessed the challenges and triumphs of aging in place. Passionate about helping older adults live safely and independently, this book is her way of sharing knowledge and experiences to empower you to make informed decisions for your safety and well-being.

Visit her website, findingafoothold.com, to learn about her podcast and coaching services and to invite her as a speaker.

Listen to the Finding A Foothold Podcast. Hear challenges that arise in caregiving and learn strategies that help reduce caregiving stress and physical work. This podcast allows caregivers to discover ways to UN-lose themselves in caregiving and enjoy more of their lives while also in a caregiving role.

Connect with Finding A Foothold at:

Email: contact@findingafoothold.com

Website: Findingafoothold.com

LinkedIn: Consuela Marshall, @Findingafoothold
Instagram: @findingafoothold
Facebook: Finding A Foothold
TikTok: @Findingafoothold

Making a Difference Together:
As part of my mission to help seniors age safely, I will donate copies of this book to my in-home clients to support their journey toward living fall-free lives. Additionally, a portion of the proceeds from this book will go to a local organization that funds respite care for family caregivers, offering them essential time away from their caregiving duties. Thank you for purchasing this book and being part of this important mission.

REFERENCES

National Council on Aging. (n.d.). Falling is not a normal part of aging. National Council on Aging. Retrieved [August 2024], from https://www.ncoa.org/older-adults/health/prevention/falls-prevention

National Institute on Aging. (n.d.). Aging in place: Growing older at home. U.S. Department of Health and Human Services. Retrieved August 10, 2024, from https://www.nia.nih.gov/health/aging-place/aging-place-growing-older-home

AARP. (2021). 2021 home and community preferences survey: A national survey of adults age 18-plus. AARP Research. https://www.aarp.org/pri/topics/livable-communities/housing/2021-home-community-preferences/

Centers for Disease Control and Prevention. (2024, May 9). Unintentional older adult fall trends. Retrieved from https://www.cdc.gov/data-research

Moreland, B. L., Kakara, R., Haddad, Y. K., Shakya, I., & Bergen, G. (2020). A Descriptive Analysis of Location of Older Adult Falls That Resulted in Emergency Department Visits in the United States, 2015. American journal of lifestyle medicine, 15(6), 590–597. https://doi.org/10.1177/1559827620942187

Moreland B, Legha J, Thomas K, Burns ER. Hip Fracture-related Emergency Department Visits, Hospitalizations, and Deaths by Mechanism of Injury Among Adults Aged 65 and Older, United States 2019. Journal of Aging and Health. 2023 Jun;35(5–6):345–355. DOI: 10.1177/08982643221132450.

Cumming, R. G., Thomas, M., Szonyi, G., Salkeld, G., O'Neill, E., Westbury, C., & Frampton, G. (1999). Home visits by an occupational therapist for assessment and modification of environmental hazards: A randomized trial of falls prevention. Journal of the American Geriatrics Society, 47(12), 1397-1402. https://doi.org/10.1111/j.1532-5415.1999.tb01556.x

PLEASE WRITE A
BOOK REVIEW.

If you found this book relatable and helpful in starting your journey to a fall-free life or providing guidance in assisting an aging parent to live fall-free in their home, your feedback would mean the world to me. I would appreciate it if you could write a review.

Why are reviews critical?
Leaving a review helps me as the author and allows more people to discover this book. Your review can make a difference in reaching others looking for practical ways to prevent falls and stay safe at home. Your review allows for book websites to prioritize the promotion of the book.

Please go to Amazon or the website where you purchased this book and:

1. Provide a star rating
2. Leave a brief review about how this book helped you or what you found most valuable.

Your review can be as simple as sharing what you learned, how you'll apply the advice, or what aspects you found most helpful.

Thank you for your support!

Made in the USA
Las Vegas, NV
06 December 2024